Tatsuki Fujimoto

I love chainsaws!

Tatsuki Fujimoto won Honorable Mention in the
November 2013 Shueisha Crown Newcomers' Awards for
his debut one-shot story *Love Is Blind*. His first series,
Fire Punch, ran for eight volumes. *Chainsaw Man* began
serialization in 2018 in *Weekly Shonen Jump*.

1

SHONEN JUMP Manga Edition

Story & Art **TATSUKI FUJIMOTO**

Translation/AMANDA HALEY
Touch-Up Art & Lettering/SABRINA HEEP
Design/JULIAN [JR] ROBINSON
Editor/ALEXIS KIRSCH

CHAINSAW MAN © 2018 by Tatsuki Fujimoto
All rights reserved.
First published in Japan in 2018 by SHUEISHA Inc., Tokyo.
English translation rights arranged by SHUEISHA Inc.

The stories, characters and incidents mentioned in this publication are entirely fictional.

Printed in Italy

Published by VIZ Media, LLC
P.O. Box 77010
San Francisco, CA 94107

20
First printing, October 2020
Twentieth printing, July 2024

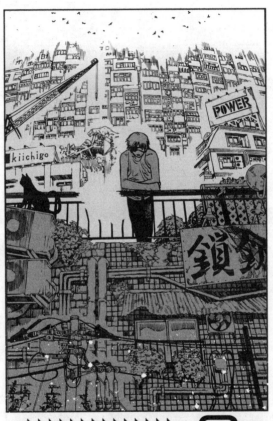

1

DOG AND CHAINSAW

Tatsuki Fujimoto

CONTENTS

...1,200,000.

THE KIDNEY I JUST SOLD...

TREE-CUTTIN'...

SOLD ONE OF MY NUTS FOR...

HOW MUCH DID IT GO FOR AGAIN?

NOT EVEN 100,000?

...300,000.

MY RIGHT EYE...

...GETS ME 60,000 YEN A MONTH.

...38,040,000 YEN.

THAT BRINGS MY DEBT DOWN TOOOOO...

LET'S GO KILL SOME-THING!

OKAY ALREADY, POCHITA. I KNOW!

Woof!

Chapter 1: Dog & Chainsaw

Chain saw man

IT'LL COME BACK FROM THE SEEDS, SO YOU SHOULD BURN IT.

THIS ONE'S A *TOMATO DEVIL*, SIR.

YOUR REWARD'S 400,000.

THIS CORPSE'LL FETCH A HEFTY SUM ON THE BLACK MARKET.

GOOD JOB, DENJI.

ONLY 70,000 LEFT FOR ME...

WHICH IS 170,000 AFTER SUB-TRACTING YOUR DEBT AND INTEREST.

WOW, *THANKS!*

THEN AFTER TAKING OUT THE FINDER'S FEE, ET CETERA...

AFTER I USE THIS TO PAY THE WATER BILL...

I'M ALREADY DOWN TO 1,800 YEN...

THAT'S FUNNY.

PLUS THE DEBTS I'VE GOT TO OTHER PEOPLE...

WE HAVE TO LIVE ON THIS FOR THE REST OF THE MONTH...

GOT NOTHING TO EAT AT HOME...

OKAY, POCHITA.

OUR MEAL FOR THE DAY IS A SINGLE SLICE OF BREAD.

WHY ARE WE EMPLOYING SOME **KID** AS A DEVIL HUNTER?

MORE ACCURATELY, HIS WORTHLESS DEAD DAD'S DEBT.

WE'RE MAKING HIM PAY BACK HIS DEBT TO US.

PLUS, WHAT'S NICE ABOUT DENJI IS HE ALWAYS DOES AS HE'S TOLD.

IS A KID WITH A PET DEVIL REALLY FIT TO BE A DEVIL HUNTER?

NO DEVIL HUNTER WORTH THEIR SALT...

...WOULD DEAL DEAD DEVIL BODIES TO THE YAKUZA, NOW WOULD THEY?

NOW WE'LL BE ABLE TO EAT FOR THE NEXT *THREE DAYS!*

ZSSHHHH

WELL, "NORMAL" IS JUST A PIPE DREAM FOR US, ANYWAY.

FEELS LIKE I'LL BE PAYING OFF MY DEBT TILL THE DAY I DIE.

APPARENTLY, IT'S NORMAL TO EAT YOUR SLICED BREAD WITH JAM ON IT.

I HEARD SOMETHING RECENTLY...

Whiiiiine

AND I'LL PROLLY NEVER GET TO GO OUT WITH A GIRL.

CAN'T ASK A GIRL OVER TO MY RUN-DOWN SHACK, AND I DON'T GOT MONEY FOR A DATE EITHER.

IF DREAMS DO COME TRUE, I WANNA HUG A GIRL BEFORE I DIE...

HHHSSS

BASTARD HUNG HIMSELF WITHOUT MAKING THIS MONTH'S PAYMENT...

OR I'LL CUT YOUR CORPSE INTO PIECES AND SELL YOU.

KID... I DON'T CARE IF YOU BEG FOR IT OR WHORE YOURSELF OUT. HAVE 700,000 YEN READY BY TOMORROW

WHEN I CAN'T SLEEP, I THINK ABOUT MY DEBT, AND THEN IT'S EVEN HARDER TO FALL ASLEEP...

SO HUNGRY I CAN'T SLEEP...

OH, I KNOW...

THIS IS WHAT I'LL DREAM OF WHEN I FALL ASLEEP TONIGHT...

...AND I'LL FALL ASLEEP IN HER ARMS...

WE'LL PLAY VIDEO GAMES IN OUR ROOM TOGETHER...

I'LL FLIRT AND STUFF WITH A GIRL.

I'LL SPREAD JAM ON SLICED BREAD AND EAT IT WITH YOU.

GOOD DREAM, RIGHT?

WOOF!!!

tak tak

TIME FOR WORK.

DENJI! GOT A DEVIL.

MY MOM... THEY SAID SHE HAD A HEART CONDITION. THAT SHE DIED COUGHING UP BLOOD...

WISH THEY'D AT LEAST LET ME DREAM....

A DEVIL SHOWED UP *HERE,* SIR?

MAYBE IT HID SOME-WHERE?

I DON'T SEE IT...

OH, UH... YES, SIR...

DENJI, BOY... WE'RE GRATEFUL TO YOU, Y'KNOW.

UH-HUH...

YOU'RE OBE-DIENT LIKE A DOG...

...AND YOU WORK FOR CHEAP TREATS LIKE ONE TOO.

THING IS... I HATE DOGS. CAN'T STAND THE SMELL.

SHM
P

SO WE DECIDED TO DO LIKE YOU AND MAKE OUR OWN DEAL WITH A DEVIL.

WE WANTED TO GET STRONGER TOO. TO MAKE MORE MONEY.

WE YAKUZA BOYS...

HEY, LITTLE DEVIL HUNTERRR!

THESE GUYS! THEY'RE SERIOUSLY STUPID! TOTAL SUCKERS!

WHEN I SAID I'D GIVE THEM MY DEVIL POWER...

...THEY BECAME MY SLAVES FREAKIN' WILLINGLY!

TOO BAD MY POWER TURNS PEOPLE INTO ZOMBIES!

CUZ I'M THE ZOMBIE DEVIL!

YOU GUYS! CUT HIM INTO PIECES AND DUMP 'IM IN THE GARBAGE!

DEVIL HUNTERS KILL US DEVILS. I HATE THEM!!

SO I KILL THEM!

I MIGHT DIE WHILE I'M FIGHTING DEVILS.

POCHITA ---

THM

P

TH
O
M

36

POCHITA

DID YOU
TAKE MY
BODY? LIKE
I TOLD
YOU TO?

...SHOW ME YOUR DREAMS.

MY WOUNDS ARE GONE...

POCHITA!

WE CUT HIM TO RIBBONS AND HE'S STILL ALIVE?!

GROSS!

I *REALLY* HATE DEVIL HUNTERS!

HUH?

YOU GUYS!! EAT THAT FREAK!!

MAYBE I'M THE SAME.

HOW COME THEY WANTED AN EVEN BETTER LIFE?

THESE GUYS ALREADY HAD PLENTY.

BUT I STILL DREAMED OF A BETTER LIFE.

I SHOULDA BEEN HAPPY AS LONG AS I HAD POCHITA.

THEN DREAMING'S NOT A BAD THING.

OH, I GET IT. EVERYBODY DREAMS. YOU CAN'T HELP IT.

IT'S NOT A BAD THING, BUT...

HE *HAS* TO STAY DEAD IF WE EAT HIM...

...TURNED INTO DEVILS DOWN TO YOUR HEARTS.

LOOKS LIKE YOU GUYS...

GOT A LIVE ONE.

HMM....

IT ISN'T HUMAN *OR* DEVIL.

YOU HAVE A PECULIAR SMELL.

DID YOU DO THIS?

topple

HOLD ME...

H...

I CAME HERE TO KILL THE ZOMBIE DEVIL.

I'M A PUBLIC SAFETY DEVIL HUNTER.

YOU HAVE TWO CHOICES.

ONE, BE KILLED BY ME AS A DEVIL.

OR TWO, BE KEPT BY ME AS A HUMAN.

FOOD...?

WHAT WOULD I GET FOR BREAKFAST?

IF YOU'RE MY PET, I'LL GIVE YOU FOOD.

Chapter 2: The Place
Where Pochita Is

gurrrrlgle

THAT'S MY STOMACH...

SORRY, UH... I'M BROKE...

LET'S GRAB SOME FOOD AT A REST STOP.

WE HAVEN'T HAD BREAKFAST EITHER.

PICK ANYTHING YOU WANT. I'LL PAY.

REALLY?!

ALSO, YOU'LL DRAW ATTENTION SHIRTLESS. PUT THIS ON.

AND BY A PRETTY GIRL, AT THAT...

THIS'S THE FIRST TIME I'VE BEEN TREATED NICE.

PEOPLE ALWAYS CALL ME DIRTY AND SMELLY. NOBODY EVER COMES NEAR ME.

I'M IN LOVE.

SURE
THING.

...A
HOT DOG!
IS THAT
OKAY?!

OH,
I'LL HAVE
UDON AND...
UDON AND...

H—

H-HELP
ME!

A D-DEVIL SNATCHED MY DAUGHTER!

MY LITTLE GIRL, IT—

WHAT HAP- PENED?

I'M A PUBLIC SAFETY DEVIL HUNTER, SIR.

IT TOOK HER INTO THE WOODS!!

IT'S DENJI!

WHAT'S YOUR NAME?

CURRY UDON'S UP!

OH... THAT'S ME.

OKAY, DENJI...

I DON'T WANT MY NOODLES TO GET SOGGY. YOU GO KILL THE DEVIL BY YOURSELF.

HUH?! UH, BUT I'M HAVING UDON TOO.

PLEASE REMAIN INSIDE THE BUILDING FOR YOUR SAFETY.

REALLY?

AN EXPERIENCED DEVIL HUNTER IS ON THE JOB, SIR. HE'LL SAVE YOUR DAUGHTER.

ONLY ANSWER WITH "YES" OR "WOOF."

DID YOU FORGET? YOU'RE MY PET.

WH... WHAT'S THAT MEAN...?

I DON'T NEED A DOG WHO SAYS "NO."

...OUR USELESS DOGS GET EUTHANIZED.

I HEARD FROM AN ACQUAINTANCE IN THE CRIME SCENE DIVISION THAT...

YES'M.

WHAT'S YOUR ANSWER?

COME ON! THE UDON'LL GET SOGGY. OFF YOU GO!

I THOUGHT SHE WAS NICE.

I EVEN LIKED HER A LITTLE.

I CAN'T BELIEVE SHE WAS THAT SCARY!

TREATIN' ME LIKE A DAMN DOG....!

Woof!

I JUST REMEMBERED POCHITA'S *DEAD...*

BLAAAH...

HA HA HA!

AH HA HA HA!

AH.

OH, PLEASE! LET THIS DEVIL GO!

WAIT, WHAT?

WHEN HE WAS HITTING ME IN THE PARKING LOT TODAY...

...THIS NICE DEVIL SAVED ME!

MY DADDY... WHEN HE HAS A BAD DAY, HE *BEATS* ME.

SO, PLEASE! DON'T KILL HIM...

OUR USELESS DOGS GET EUTHANIZED.

I WAS BUDDIES WITH A DEVIL TOO. I KNOW...

...THERE ARE GOOD DEVILS.

HUH?

HEY... WANNA RUN AWAY TOGETHER? THE THREE OF US...?

BUT IF I LET THIS DEVIL GO, THEY'RE GONNA KILL ME.

SO DO YOU WANNA RUN AWAY...?

clasp

Ан на
на на на!

CAN
WE...?

AH
HA!

WE
TOTALLY
CAN!

AH HA
HA HA
HA HA
HA HA!

HA
HA
HA...

HA
HA...
HUH?

AH HA HA HA
HA HA HA HA!

topple

UH-OH.

SHE SMELLS GOOD...

YOU OKAY?

whump

SORRY... I END UP CUTTING MY OWN BODY WITH THE CHAINSAWS TOO...

LOOKS LIKE I LOSE TOO MUCH BLOOD AND GET FAINT...

HOW DID YOUR BODY END UP LIKE THAT?

MY PET DEVIL BECAME MY HEART.

UNBELIEVABLE, RIGHT?

THAT POCHITA DIED FOR ME...

I DON'T WANNA BELIEVE IT EITHER.

HISTORICALLY SPEAKING, YOUR CONDITION HAS VERY FEW PRECEDENTS.

SO FEW IT HASN'T EVEN BEEN NAMED.

SO I CAN TELL.

I HAVE AN ESPECIALLY GOOD NOSE.

I BELIEVE YOU.

YOUR BODY HAS *TWO* SCENTS. HUMAN *AND* DEVIL.

AND NOT IN THE POETIC SENSE...

YOUR BEST FRIEND IS STILL ALIVE INSIDE YOU.

OKAY...

WOW...

THAT'S A HUGE RELIEF!

I'LL EAT THAT UDON ...

I CA—

I can't.

CAN YOU FEED YOUR-SELF?

YOU LOOK UNSTEADY.

gurgle

GOOD?

Woof!

YOU REALLY ARE LIKE A DOG.

HARD TO BELIEVE YOU ACTUALLY ENJOYED THAT SOGGY UDON...

WHAT A GOOD BOY.

MAKIMA.

WHAT'S YOUR NAME...?

HEY, UH!

WHAT TYPE OF GUY DO YOU LIKE?

W....

MISS MAKIMA ...

HMMM...

Chapter 3: Arrival in Tokyo

WHAT TYPE OF GUY DO YOU LIKE?

SOMEONE LIKE THIS BOY NAMED DENJI.

ME TOO... I LIKE YOU TOO, MISS MAKIMA...

DENJI! OVER HERE!

YES ?!

DENJI.

ONCE YOU'RE CHANGED, I'LL INTRODUCE YOU TO ONE OF YOUR COLLEAGUES.

WE TYPICALLY WORK IN UNIFORM. PUT THIS ON.

FOR TODAY, TAG ALONG WITH HIM.

THIS IS *AKI HAYA-KAWA.*

HE'S THREE YEARS YOUR SENIOR HERE.

OF COURSE NOT.

I'M NOT WORKING WITH YOU, MISS MAKIMA?

Nooo! Miss Maki-maaa!!

WE'RE GOING ON PATROL.

YOU AND MISS MAKIMA ARE IN COMPLETELY DIFFERENT LEAGUES.

CRA
SH

WHU

IF YOU SHOW UP TOMORROW, I'LL GIVE YOU ANOTHER THRASHING.

YOU SHOULD QUIT.

MAYBE MY KINDNESS ISN'T GETTING THROUGH TO YOU...

WHAT'S YOUR PROB- LEM...?

THE ONLY ONES STILL ALIVE ARE THOSE WHO HAVE STRONG CONVICTION.

AMONG MY PEERS, THE ONES WHO BECAME DEVIL HUNTERS JUST FOR THE MONEY GOT KILLED BY DEVILS. ALL OF THEM.

THE PEOPLE WHO GO INTO THIS JOB FOR SHALLOW REASONS END UP *DEAD*, KID.

DiNG DiiiNG.

LEMME GUESS. YOU BECAME A DEVIL HUNTER CUZ YOU'VE GOT YOUR EYE ON MAKIMA?

THEN I WAS RIGHT TO BEAT YOU UP.

PTOO

SPLAT

...YOU GOT SCARED OF A DEVIL AND RAN AWAY.

I'LL DO YOU A FAVOR AND TELL MAKIMA...

MY LIFE ISN'T MINE ALONE.

ACTUALLY, I TAKE THAT BACK.

GFF!

DO NG

YOU JUST WANT HER FOR YOURSELF!!

HUH?! WHAT GIVES?!

...HAS NO PLACE LIKING MAKIMA!

A THUG LIKE YOU...

THUD

YOU... SERIOUSLY...

CRAP.

...ONLY AIM FOR...

...THE BALLS...

A ***TESTICLE DEVIL*** ATTACKED HIS BALLS.

THAT'S A LIE... HE MADE THAT UP...

CAN YOU GET ALONG?

SO WHAT DO YOU THINK?

HMMM.

THIS GUY IS SCUM...

NOT A CHANCE.

I'M GLAD YOU GUYS ARE HITTING IT OFF.

THIS THUG?! REALLY?!

Squad?

BUT WE ALREADY HAVE SO MANY TROUBLE-MAKERS AS IT IS!

IF WE ADD ANY MORE WEIRDOS...

I'M PUTTING DENJI IN YOUR SQUAD, HAYAKAWA.

THAT I'D TRY OPERATING IT WITH A UNIQUE EXPERIMENTAL SETUP.

I TOLD YOU WHEN WE CREATED YOUR SQUAD, DIDN'T I?

JUST WHO IS THIS GUY?

yawn

DENJI HERE IS HUMAN, BUT HE CAN TURN INTO A DEVIL.

ARE YOU SERIOUS?

I'VE ONLY HEARD FLIMSY RUMORS ABOUT CASES LIKE THAT...

HOW DO YOU LIKE THAT?! BADASS, RIGHT?!

DENJI IS SPECIAL.

SO IT'S BEEN DECIDED THAT WE'LL TREAT HIM AS A SPECIAL CASE.

IF DENJI EVER QUITS OR DISOBEYS ORDERS...

...HE'LL BE PUT DOWN AS A DEVIL.

IT MEANS WE'LL BE WORKING TOGETHER UNTIL DEATH DO US PART.

WAIT... WHAT'S THAT MEAN?

FYI, THEY TOLD ME I CAN KILL YOU IF YOU RUN AWAY.

TURNS OUT YOU'RE GONNA LIVE WITH ME SO WE CAN KEEP AN EYE ON YOU.

IS MAKIMA A BAD PERSON?

HEY...

THEN IS SHE A GOOD PERSON?

IF YOU'RE A DEVIL, JUST BE GRATEFUL WE'RE LETTING YOU LIVE.

WE'RE DEVIL HUNTERS, REMEMBER?

IF YOU THINK SO, THEN GIVE UP ON HER.

OF COURSE SHE'S A GOOD PERSON...

I OWE HER MY LIFE...

Chain

saw

man

Chapter 4: Power

TA-DAA

AND THE ULTIMATE BREAD IS READY!

STRAWBERRY JAM, PLUM JAM, MARMALADE AAAND...

...BUTTER AND HONEYYY AND... SHAKE SOME CINNAMON ON THERE TOO.

Mm!

PAID DAYS OFF, HUH-HUMM HUH-HUMM-HUM HUH-HUMM HUH-HUMM HUM!

UNION JOB, HUMM HUH-HUMM HUH HUH HUH HUH-HUMM!

You're taking too Long in the bath!

bam bam bam

Don't sleep on the toilet!

WE'VE GOT A *FIEND* INSIDE AN EAST NERIMA RESIDENCE.

CIVILIAN EVACUATION AND LOCKDOWN OF THE SCENE IS COMPLETE AT THIS TIME.

MR. HAYAKAWA, IS THAT A NEWBIE WITH YOU?

WE'LL LET YOU DEVIL HUNTERS HANDLE THE REST.

THE FIEND TARGET IS HOLED UP IN A ROOM ON THE SECOND FLOOR.

WHAT? DIDN'T YOU LEARN ANYTHING IN SCHOOL?

NOPE, DIDN'T GO TO SCHOOL.

HEY, WHAT'S A FIEND?

THEN AREN'T I ONE?

OHH.

OH REALLY? UH...

NO.

THEIR HEADS HAVE DISTINCT SHAPES.

A DEVIL THAT'S TAKEN OVER A PERSON'S CORPSE...

THAT'S A FIEND.

WELL, YOU'LL UNDERSTAND WHEN YOU SEE ONE.

TURN INTO A DEVIL. SHOW ME YOUR POWER.

I'LL DECIDE WHETHER YOU'RE USEFUL OR NOT.

YOU KILL THIS ONE.

FIENDS HAVE THE DEVIL'S PERSONALITY.

BANG

LISTEN UP. DON'T YOU FORGET THIS.

FIENDS ARE BONA FIDE DEVILS TOO.

A DEVIL HUNTER SHOULDN'T BE SYMPATHIZING WITH DEVILS.

MY ENTIRE FAMILY WAS KILLED BY A DEVIL RIGHT BEFORE MY EYES.

THE COPS DOWN THERE? I'VE GONE DRINKING WITH THEM BEFORE.

THEY'RE RISKING THEIR LIVES TO DO THEIR JOBS, TO PROTECT THEIR WIVES AND KIDS.

EVERYONE IS SERIOUS ABOUT THIS BUT YOU.

I WANT TO KILL DEVILS IN WAYS THAT CAUSE THEM TO SUFFER AS MUCH AS POSSIBLE.

WHAT DO YOU WANT? TO BE FRIENDS WITH THEM?

CUZ I DON'T HAVE ANY FRIENDS...

IF THERE ARE DEVILS I COULD BE FRIENDS WITH, THEN YEAH, I DO.

I'LL REMEMBER THOSE WORDS...

SLAM

BLAAAH... HE SURE HAS A SHORT TEMPER...

THE TRUTH IS, I JUST DIDN'T WANNA GET BLOOD ON THESE DIRTY MAGAZINES...

CUZ WITH THE CHAINSAWS, BLOOD ENDS UP SPRAYING ALL OVER.

I DID YOU A FAVOR KILLING YOU QUICK, SO I'M TAKING THESE!

ALL RIGHT! Sexiness confirmed!

flip

SHOW ME YOUR DREAMS.

I'M SERIOUS ABOUT THIS TOO, POCHITA.

I'M LIVING A DREAM LIFE, JUST LIKE IN OUR CONTRACT, AREN'T I?

HE'S STILL CHASING HIS.

IT'S JUST THAT I'VE ALREADY CROSSED THE FINISH LINE TO MY DREAM.

WITH A PRETTY GIRL CLOSE BY...

I GET TO BATHE EVERY DAY.

AND EAT GOOD FOOD.

FOR THE GUYS BELOW, IT'S PROTECTING THEIR FAMILIES.

I BET HIS ULTIMATE GOAL IS A REVENGE THING.

I HAVE A FULL LIFE NOW... BUT IT DOES KINDA FEEL LIKE SOMETHING'S MISSING.

WAS THERE SOMETHING ELSE? MY REAL, TRUE GOAL...?

DOES MAKIMA HAVE ONE TOO?

DOES MAKIMA ALSO...

I WANNA TOUCH SOME BOOBS...

BUT IF IT'S BOOBS...

JUMPING STRAIGHT TO SLEEPING WITH A WOMAN WOULD BE TOUGH FOR ME...

IF IT'S BOOBS, IF I'VE GOT A STRONG WILL AND INITIATIVE, COULDN'T I TOUCH THEM...?

I GAVE UP ON IT FOREVER AGO CUZ I THOUGHT IT WAS IMPOSSIBLE FOR ME...

BUT I HAVE A DECENT JOB NOW. COULDN'T I DO IT?

SO THAT'S WHAT HE MEANT! I'VE FOUND IT, DUDE...

WHAT I'M SERIOUS ABOUT!

MY GOAL!

IT'S....!

EVERYONE IS SERIOUS ABOUT THIS BUT YOU.

A BUDDY ---?

MAKIMA SAID SHE LIKED ME... BUT...

...IF I ASK TO TOUCH HER CHEST, THERE'S A CHANCE SHE'LL HATE ME...

I'M PAIRING YOU UP WITH A BUDDY STARTING TODAY.

PERFECT TIMING— LOOKS LIKE YOUR BUDDY'S HERE.

IN PUBLIC SAFETY, FOR SMALL-SCALE MISSIONS, PATROLLING AND SO ON, WE ACT IN PAIRS FOR SAFETY'S SAKE.

BE CARE-FUL...

SHE'S A FIEND.

Chainsaw man

Chapter 5:
A Way to Touch Some Boobs

HUMAN! HURRY UP AND LET ME KILL SOMETHING!

I THIRST FOR BLOOD!

I CAN FORGIVE SOME CRAZINESS AS LONG AS SHE'S PRETTY...

THE ISSUE IS HOW I'M GONNA TOUCH THOSE BOOBS...

BUT POWER HAS HIGH MENTAL FACULTIES, SO I PUT HER IN HAYAKAWA'S SQUAD.

FIENDS ARE TARGETS FOR EXTERMINATION, SAME AS DEVILS.

HER HORNS WILL ATTRACT ATTENTION, SO ONLY PATROL PLACES WITH LITTLE TRAFFIC.

We're with Public Safety Devil Extermination Special Division 4, sirrrs.

IF YOU RUN INTO ANY CIVILIAN DEVIL HUNTERS, OR GET QUESTIONED BY THE POLICE...

IF YOU TELL THEM THAT AND SHOW THEM YOUR BADGE, THEY SHOULD SCOWL AND LEAVE YOU ALONE.

AS I'VE SAID BEFORE, PUBLIC SAFETY DEVIL EXTERMINATION SPECIAL DIVISION 4 IS AN EXPERIMENTAL SQUAD.

IF IT CAN'T DELIVER RESULTS, THE HIGHER-UPS MIGHT BREAK IT UP AT ANY TIME.

YOU TWO KNOW WHAT WILL HAPPEN TO YOU THEN, RIGHT?

THERE aren't any Devils at all!

THEN HOW ARE WE GOING TO DELIVER RESULTS?!

WAIT, WHAT?!

THE NOBODY DEVILS ALL FLEE FROM MY SCENT, I'M SURE!

BEFORE I BECAME A FIEND, I WAS A GREATLY FEARED DEVIL!

LIKELY BECAUSE OF *ME*!

HE'S THE ONE WHO PAIRED YOU TWO UP.

IF YOU HAVE ANY QUESTIONS, ASK HAYAKAWA.

HE TEAMED ME UP WITH POWER TO KEEP ME FROM SHOWING WHAT I GOT.

HE'S TRYING TO FORCE ME OUT!

THAT JERK... HE SET ME UP, DIDN'T HE?!

I SMELL BLOOD!!

HEY! WHOA, WHOA, WHOA! WHERE DO YOU THINK YOU'RE GOING?!

FIGHT TIME! FIGHT TIME! BATTLE TIME!

SHE'S FAST!

POWER, SINCE YOU WERE THE *BLOOD DEVIL* BEFORE YOU BECAME A FIEND, BATTLING USING BLOOD IS YOUR SPECIALTY...

...BUT YOU'RE SO EXCITABLE... MAYBE YOU WEREN'T CUT OUT TO BE A DEVIL HUNTER?

Exci–?!

HUH ?!

THIS GUY SAID TO KILL IT, HE DID!

THISH–

HUH...?!

I-I CAN!

CAN YOU BE QUIET?

GOOD GIRL, POWER.

HONESTLY, I DON'T REALLY CARE WHICH OF YOU WAS AT FAULT.

I WANT TO SEE BIG THINGS FROM YOU TWO.

I'LL SH—! SH-SHOW YOU!

DO YOU THINK YOU CAN SHOW ME THAT?

MAYBE THIS ISN'T THE TIME TO BE THINKING ABOUT TOUCHING BOOBS.

MEOOOW!

STILL, I CAN'T WORK WITH SOME LIAR CHICK...

BUT IF WE KEEP SCREWING UP, IT'LL BE WAY WORSE THAN NOT GETTING TO HAVE SOFT DRINKS ANYMORE!

GETTING TO HAVE SOFT DRINKS IS, LIKE, A DREAM COME TRUE TO ME.

FOR A CAT? THAT'S STUPID!

I'D DO ANYTHING TO TOUCH SOME BOOBS THOUGH.

I DOUBT YOU'D UNDERSTAND SUCH SENTIMENT FOR THE LIKES OF A CAT.

IF I COULD JUST GET MEOWY BACK FROM THAT DEVIL, I'D DO ANYTHING— EVEN ALLY WITH A HUMAN!

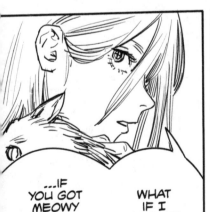

...IF YOU GOT MEOWY BACK FROM THAT DEVIL FOR ME?

WHAT IF I SAID I'D LET YOU TOUCH MY CHEST...

HMM ---

OH, BUT IF IT WAS A *DOG*, I MIGHT GET IT...

SURE ENOUGH, I CAN'T COMPREHEND HUMANS.

HOW DARE...

...THEY KIDNAP A POOR CAT!!

OHH?!

THAT DAMN DEVIL!

OHH?

C h a i n

s a w

m a n

YOU CAN'T EVEN GO OUT ON YOUR OWN?

NOPE. I WAS SO BORED BEING IN HERE ALL THE TIME.

BE BACK BY FIVE O'CLOCK!

YOUR DAY-LEAVE REQUEST FOR THE FIEND POWER IS APPROVED.

Chapter 6: Service

THE PROBLEM IS THAT ONLY *YOU* CAN FIGHT IT.

IF IT SEES *ME*, IT'LL USE MEOWY AS A SHIELD.

THEN IT WOULD BE CHECK-MATE!

I KNOW WHERE TO FIND THE DEVIL WHO TOOK MEOWY!

CUZ HE'S ALIVE INSIDE ME, RIGHT IN HERE!

I CAN'T EVER PET HIM AGAIN, BUT IT'S OKAY.

HUMANS ARE SO FOOLISH!

I HAD A PET TOO. THIS DEVIL NAMED POCHITA.

THAT MEANS POCHITA DIED, DOES IT NOT?

THE DEAD HAVE NO LIFE!

"THEY'RE IN MY HEART" OR WHATEVER— THAT'S PATHETIC CONSOLATION!

SAY WHAT?

Chapter 6: Service

YEAH, YEAH... YOU'RE SO RIGHT.

THERE'S NOOO WAY I CAN BE FRIENDS WITH THIS CHICK.

THE SOVIET WAR HAWKS ARE GETTING LOUDER OVER THE AMERICAN MATTER.

WE'RE ALSO HEARING RUMORS THAT THEY'RE USING DEVILS FOR MILITARY PURPOSES.

MAKIMA... ARE THE DOGS IN THE SQUAD WE GAVE YOU COMING ALONG...?

WE CAN ONLY PRAY THAT THE DEVILS REMAIN JAPAN'S ONLY ENEMIES.

I HAVE ONE DOG THAT'S PROMISING...

...AND ONE THAT'S INTERESTING.

A PUPPY I RECENTLY TOOK IN.

INTERESTING...?

BE SURE NOT TO GET ATTACHED.

YOUR JOB IS TO TRAIN DOGS AND USE THEM.

SL AM

WHY DO YOU HAVE SUCH HIGH HOPES FOR HIM?

ALL DEVILS ARE BORN WITH A NAME.

DENJI IS DISGUSTING. THERE'S NOTHING INTERESTING ABOUT HIM.

THE MORE THAT NAME IS FEARED, THE MORE POWERFUL THE DEVIL ITSELF.

BUT WHAT IF THERE WAS A *CAR DEVIL?* THAT CONJURES UP THE MENTAL IMAGE OF GETTING RUN OVER AND DYING, SO THAT MIGHT BE STRONG.

COFFEE HAS NO SCARY MENTAL IMAGE WHATSOEVER. IF THERE WAS A *COFFEE DEVIL,* IT WOULD PROBABLY BE WEAK.

DENJI CAN TURN INTO THE *CHAINSAW DEVIL.*

I REALLY DO THINK THAT'S INTEREST-ING.

IT'S INTERESTING AND NOTHING MORE. HE'S USE-LESS.

HE ISN'T FIT FOR PUBLIC SAFETY.

BUT HIM, HE SAID ALL HE WANTS IS TO LIVE THE EASY LIFE.

ONLY PEOPLE WITH GOALS OR CONVICTION SERVE IN PUBLIC SAFETY.

NOT TO MENTION HE THINKS YOU CAN BECOME *FRIENDS* WITH DEVILS.

HE'S STILL A BRAT.

JUST SOME BRAT.

'TIS THAT HOUSE!

MEOWY AND THE DEVIL ARE IN THERE!

HUUUH... THEN LET'S GET OUR BUTTS OVER THERE.

YEAH, I CAN TURN INTO CHAINSAWS!

OHH? GO CHAIN-SAWS?

MAN, I DON'T REALLY WANNA GO ALL CHAINSAWS ON IT CUZ I'LL GET FAINT...

HUMAN JESTS ARE SO UNAMUSING!

YEAH? WHAT IS IT?

HUH?

STORY?

OHH? WAS THAT MY STORY?

ISN'T IT GONNA USE YOUR CAT AS A HOSTAGE IF YOU SHOW UP?

YOU CAN'T COME THIS CLOSE WITH ME, RIGHT?

HE'S A FOOL, BUT HE HAD GOOD INTUITION...

UGH!

UHN...

SL AM

I HAD TO WAIT THAT LONG TILL I COULD FINALLY GET OUTSIDE TOO!

DON'T COMPLAIN!

I THOUGHT YOU'D RUN AWAY...

YOU MADE ME WAIT FOR QUITE SOME TIME, BLOOD DEVIL...

GAH!

THIS INFERNAL WOUND FORCED ME TO HIDE MY GRAND SELF!

LOOK AT MY ARM, HUMAN! YOU DAMN HUMANS DID THIS TO ME!

LIKE I CARE, IDIOT!

...SO I'LL HEAL IT WITH HUMAN BLOOD!

HUMANS CARVED THIS WOUND UPON ME...

MY MEAL BARKS!

MAKE-UP...

...AND MEDI-CINE...

THE SMELL OF CIGA-RETTES...

NOW THAT'S NOT A BAD SMELL.

I'VE SETTLED ON CHILDREN TO CLEANSE MY PALATE!

BAT
DEVIL
!!

NOW
GIVE
MEOWY
BACK!

I BROUGHT
YOU A
HUMAN AS
PROMISED!

AH, YES...
WAS
THAT THE
DEAL?

HRRM
?

FOR A CAT, YOU SMELL TASTY!

MEOWY! YOUR NAME SHALL BE MEOWY!

METHINKS I'LL FATTEN YOU UP A LITTLE BEFORE I EAT YOU!

YOU'RE ALL SKIN AND BONES...

Mrow!

lick

SPssh

HURRY AND GROW BIG!

I'M EAGER TO KILL YOU!

Meooooow.

gulp

YOU SAID
YOU CAN'T
PET POCHITA
ANYMORE...

THERE WAS THIS ONE TIME POCHITA WENT MISSING.

BUT WHEN I GOT HOME, POCHITA WAS THERE WAITING FOR ME, CRYING.

I THOUGHT HE'D BEEN EATEN BY A DEVIL.

I LOOKED ALL OVER TOWN AND STILL COULDN'T FIND 'IM.

POCHITA WASN'T THERE WHEN I WOKE UP.

I REMEMBER BEING SO RELIEVED THAT WE FELL ASLEEP TOGETHER RIGHT ON THE SPOT.

...HOW DID SHE FEEL WHEN SHE WENT TO SLEEP AT NIGHT?

AFTER MEOWY GOT TAKEN BY A DEVIL....

TO BE CONTINUED...

Chain
saw

man

YOU'RE READING THE WRONG WAY!

Chainsaw Man reads from right to left, starting in the upper-right corner. Japanese is read from right to left, meaning that action, sound effects and word-balloon order are completely reversed from English order.